strong hearts still break

by

c.r. Elliott

ISBN: 9798645960711

for my mother,

who taught me to have a voice

&

my wife,

who helped me find it

also by c.r. Elliott

sugar, honey, ice & tea

visit him on Instagram

@c.r.elliott_poetry

drapetomania

(n.) an overwhelming urge to run away

evanescent

(adj.) soon passing out of sight, memory, or existence; quickly fading or disappearing

ephemeral

(adj.) lasting for a very short time

<u>blind to the future</u>

don't starve yourself of love
just because you got hurt in the past;
it is the most selfish thing you can do.
you get hurt,
you take the pain,
turn it into strength and growth
and you move on.
looking back on the past
will only make you blind to the future.

fighting alone

how much more pain
do you have to endure
to realize
that you are the only one
fighting for something
that has died a long time ago?

if it was true to begin with
and as real as it felt
then you wouldn't have to
fight it alone.

growth

i admire you
for surviving that bad relationship,
for leaving those bad memories,
for outgrowing those past experiences.
i adore you for who you became
and for how far you came.

strength, vol I

you turned pain into strength,
bad experiences into memories,
scars into healed wounds.
you are stronger than you know,
i just hope you see it too.

balance

it is hard to find balance
between the heart and mind
in what they say
as often
they pull in different directions
while one thinks rational
the other dictates emotional
and sometimes we go down a dark path
for the right reasons
we just don't see the lesson
until we come back to the light again

focus on forward

stop fixating on bad memories
and troubled experiences
they shaped you into what you are today
strong and wise
enough to take on the whole world

heart in depth

the last thing you need
is to lose your place
to leave your heart in depth
just to make them happy

only the best

never settle for someone
who is not willing to commit
just because you are afraid
to be alone

hard-learned lesson

don't worry about heartache

some people come in your life
just to show what and where
not to look for
love & happiness

you know better

you can forgive
but don't let them back in

in the unknown

if you want change
you must stop accepting
what you are used to

- growth is in the unknown

heart of a warrior

there is a wilderness
inside her heart
waiting to be freed
clawing her way up
from the dark well
she was thrown
she will not surrender
she will not succumb
she is a warrior
and this is only half
of what she can do

strength, vol II

she's the kind of woman
you can throw to the wolves
but tomorrow she will come back
as a leader of the whole pack

hoping

i hope you find someone
that will make you feel
all your past relationships
were not worthy of the title
LOVE

haunted

the way your presence
still lingers near
years after you left
like a ghost haunting my walls
is proof just how real
my love for you truly was
and even after i healed
the scars remained
reminding me what was
and what can never be again

letting go, part I.

it is okay to feel lost
sometimes we must let
the dark take us
so we can find our way
towards the light again

sad song

she's just a sad song
but that doesn't mean
she isn't beautiful
...
she sings from the heart
it may not always be beautiful
but every note is real
just like her

tired

you are strong
enough to carry
the whole world
on your shoulders
even when the weight
breaks your bones
...
you are strong
and with your heavy soul
it's okay to be tired

free of you

when you lose her
you'll begin to wonder
...
when she's free of you
she won't even have to think
that the past is a memory
a hard lesson learned
but the future is bright
and won't be the same

fighting on

her heart was broken
shattered beyond repair
but nothing is ever truly broken
if the mind refuses to give in

dark cage

break free of his chains
before the dark in his heart
plagues yours as well
and robs you of your light

soul eaters

the men that take you
when you are lonely
pray on your fears
and make false promises
are a disease
that will eat away at your light
until you are left
nothing but a broken shell

stolen light

i know the fights you go through at night
the restlessness of your heart
trying so desperately to survive
without the light that was taken from you
breathing on stale air
that leaves you numb to the bones
from trusting the one who
you gave it your all
just to feel free and happy
yet they took it without question
and cast you aside in the dark
not knowing the harm that they caused
for they are walking in stolen light
not even aware
that without your presence
it will burn out
and leave them longing
for something
that was never even theirs

lock the door

i was standing here
with my heart in my hands
prepared to give it to you
yet you walked away
thinking i was unworthy of your love
but when i gave to another
you ran back to me
thinking my arms would still be open
and my heart waiting for you.
i am not your second choice,
your hopeless effort
when you failed somewhere else.
you made me think
i was unworthy of you
but now i see
that you were unworthy of me.
i just needed to step aside
to finally see
the poison you became to me.

preying on love

you only loved me
when you needed me
you played me
since you knew
i was starving of love
as my heart was empty
longing to feel whole again
you never truly loved me
as i truly loved you

feed on the starving

you never loved me
the way i loved you
you were only with me
because you knew my heart was starving
but in all our time together
you were the one that was fed
taking what little was of me

refusal

you have no right
to refuse giving love
just because you do not have
the capacity for it
don't take
if you don't know
how to give
just to make yourself
feel better

self-worth

i loved you
when we were together
but i love you more
now that we're apart
for showing me
what i am worth
and teaching me
where not to find it

outcome of starvation

they starved you of affection
told words of love without meaning
showed emotion without depth
and now you stand here
doing the same to me
thinking that it is right
just because it is all you know
even when fully aware
which road it leads you
and how it makes you feel

just for tonight

just for tonight
let go and be free
forget about the troubles
and thoughts
that weigh you down
• • • ◊ • • •
just for tonight
it is only you

growing

they tell you empty words
and broken promises
but that is a tale
that they told you before
and while they were lying
you were growing

stranger

i saw her crying alone
sitting on the bench at night
clutching her phone
her face wet of sadness
not knowing how much
was it tears
and how much was it rain

i watched you from afar
my heart broken
seeing yours that way
under the night's sky
thinking
*"how can someone
so beautiful
be so miserable?"*
but there you were
shattered to pieces
not knowing if you can
put yourself back again

foolish kings/righteous rulers

there are false kings
fighting to sit on thrones
they do not deserve
and wear crowns
stolen from those
who are more worthy
to the kingdom
that is your heart

expectations

you can't take a wolf home
expecting it to be a dog.
everyone loves a bad boy
but know what you are bringing home.

wilderness

there is a wilderness inside her heart,
a mighty lioness in the shape of a cat.
do not underestimate
what you don't understand.

broken births beauty, part I.

she fought her demons
and while her scars were showing
she never looked more beautiful

scars as wings

she is a warrior
who fought for years
with the demons
that plagued her mind
and darkened her soul
but in the end
she never looked more
like an angel
when she wore her
scars like wings

step aside

sometimes,
we must get away from the light
to see just how much
we shine in the dark

late wishing

how i wish for us both
to knew the meaning of forever
before we promised it
to each other

broken fragments

i am still finding broken fragments
from a once broken heart
with bitter memories resurfacing
as my soul becomes
a house with ghosts in the walls

different intentions

it is sad
looking back on it now
realizing
you were looking
for a temporary shelter
while i was searching
for a home

weight

can you imagine
the weight i carry
when i let you go
to be with someone else
knowing that the only thing i want
is for you to be happy
even if i am not the one
responsible for it

<u>(never) be mine</u>

i knew
you could never be mine
right from the start
but the feeling
still weighing me down
feels like i can sink a ship
with my heavy heart

opposite directions

for the longest time
it took me to realize
that as much as we were
both walking on the same path
we were walking in opposite directions
till the moment came
when we were too far apart
separated by the distance of our hearts
to find our way to each other again

not enough

you lingered in my past
while i focused on our future
and still you come and say
i haven't done enough
when all i truly gave you
was a possibility of letting go
and actually becoming happy

reminder, part I.

leave them in the past
where they broke
all their promises
and betrayed your trust
and remind yourself
why you walked away

dangerous thing

love
is a dangerous
but beautiful thing
especially when
i pass it from my hands
to yours
without knowing
what will happen
but still hoping
it will be returned back to me

self-made prison

you have built walls around yourself
to protect from the past hurt
so no one can get in anymore
but the very walls that protect you
you now grew to hate
as they surround you with fear
of what you think
can't come true for you
alienated from the world
that you crave
but afraid to look

clash of seasons

a snowflake fallen from the sky
caught by your warm palms
will melt in the bitter air
so why do you think
his cold heart
can carry your warm spirit

building sandcastles

i was a child
that built
sandcastles of hope
on a beach
and you were
the violent wave
that wiped it
from existence

crumbling walls

stop looking
for a permanent home
in temporary people
and still question
why do the walls
crumble down
so easily

beautiful rose

she is a beautiful rose
and while they're mistaking
her breakable petals for weakness
they're blind
to the strength of her thorns

in the middle

how do you expect to heal
in you're caught in the middle
of getting over it
and still wanting them back

power

your heart
carries the soul
of a wolf
and with it
the strength
of the wild
and the power
to make the moon listen

worth the chase

he was never worth the chase
but you were always
worth the effort

fragile as sand

i fought so hard
for us to stay whole,
but one heart
can't beat for two.
so i choked
so we could breathe,
but in the end
my lungs weren't strong enough
for the air needed
to keep us alive
and as much as i hated
we grew apart
and as much as i tried
you still slipped away
like sand through my fingers.

reminder, part II.

stop playing out
all the lives
that could have been
if you stayed
and remember
the actions
and words
that made you
walk away

self-love filler

you said your absence
from my life
will make me empty
when in reality
it gave me space
to fill it with love
which i was deprived from you

within you

there is a power living within you,
magic breathing beneath your bones,
courage beating in your heart
and strength running through your blood.

know your value

don't let rusted copper
diminish the worth
of a diamond in the rough

remind the reason

let go of the illusion
that it could be any different
when deep down you know
the reason you walked away
from the toxic situation

knowing worth

a rich man is unimpressed
with a diamond
while a poor man
knows the worth
he holds in his hands

light inside

and despite everything
she took their sharp words
and found a light inside her
bright enough to cast a shadow
on those who put her there
in the first place

rare

don't waste your time
with fools who can't see
just how rare you are

<u>hero</u>

don't you see
the hero that you
are looking for
has been with you
all along
living inside your heart
fighting battles
you never even knew existed

reminder, part III.

you can regret your heartaches
but in no way do you repeat them

growing ghosts

stop planting seeds of pain
in soil of grief
expecting it to produce
anything other than ghosts of the past

falling together/better apart

just like the sun and the moon
we needed to grow apart
in order to shine brighter inside

war

i tell myself
that you were not
meant to stay
and were right
to walk away
but then quietly
go to war with myself

loving myself

i gave you my love
and you ignored it
you promised the world
and i fell for it
but now i'm choosing
to love myself
because i deserve it

after the storm

and after the storm
the clouds opened up
and the soil grew
from the raindrops fallen
while the sun
shines a light
on another beautiful day

bitter lies dipped in honey

don't fall for words
dipped in honey
with hint of poison
and chosen so wisely
that plucks the heartstrings
and preys on vulnerability
to make you fall in love
so blindly

<u>falling</u>

just because you're falling
with nowhere to land
does not mean
you don't have a choice
where you're going
or what your life
is going to be

broken things of beauty

if you ask me
broken things
are even more beautiful
when the light
radiates through the cracks
showing not only scars
but the strength
accepting and carrying them
like they were part of you
to begin with

creating a home

first you must create
a home in yourself
before you start
letting people in

half-full

my dear,
you are like the moon;
worth of admiration
even when you are far
from being full.

surroundings

your loneliness
isn't from lack of company
but a product
of lacking a connection
with those
who surround you

compass

your compass isn't broken.
being lost
is just the place
where you need to start.

<u>evolution</u>

when a bird
flies over an ocean
with no place to land
it learns how to swim
in order to rest its wings
so she can fill
her feathers with air
and take flight
to the open sky
once again

lost places

stop looking for a road
which isn't there anymore
to go back to a person
who isn't waiting anymore

no wonder

she was constantly burning
from lack of love
and always freezing
from the feeling of loneliness
and yet they still wonder
why a woman born from violence
is just not ready to be touched

<u>her</u>

the mountains
will crumble
at her feet
at the sight
of what she became

the stars
will fall
out of alignment
just to witness
her new strength

the rain will start
falling from the sky
and the flowers
will start to grow
from the ground
in her name

the moon
will hide its light
behind the clouds
and wolves
will howl
for her

the art of letting go

sometimes we make mistakes
so we can learn
the art of l
       e
      t
      t
      i
       n
        g

         g
          o

the power of love

never underestimate
the power of love
as it controls the heart
to feel heavy when empty
and weightless when full

new year's resolution

your new year's resolution should be
to be fluent in self-worth
so by the end of the year
your heart is so full of self-love
that you know your worth
like it's your mother tongue

choosing yourself

never apologize
for choosing yourself
and giving the love you deserve
as it is the best chapter
of your story

<u>fairytales</u>

boy,
you read too many fairytales
that you started living in one
because i am not the damsel you seek
but the wolf you run away from

-scream it from the heart

the right audience

i was wishing
to one day wake up
and matter to the world
until the day finally came
when i realized
i was the only
audience i needed

no regrets

never regret your dark days
as they bring balance to your life.
if the sun shone all day
you would find yourself in drought.
you need those few rainy days,
just enough dark clouds
so you can grow
and plant new seeds.

letting go, part II.

love is an open sea
and to save yourself
from drowning
you must stop the fight
and let go
so the current can carry you

reminder, part IV.

stop giving
the wrong people
the right
pieces of you

growing in storms

i think back
to all the memories
that brew storms up above
and the rain that soaked
my heavy heart
but when the clouds cleared
i saw just how much
i grew from it

cherish your spark

don't burn yourself
just to light a flame in him

helpless

it breaks my heart
seeing someone
so beautiful
be so miserable
and not knowing
how to stop the tears
from falling
and the heart
from breaking

late rise

there are days
when the sun rises late
but in the end
still lights up the day
to a perfect moment
don't worry,
your time will come.

broken births beauty, part II.

your broken
only makes your smile
that much stronger,
your eyes
that much deeper,
and your heart
that much warmer.

planting seeds

i planted seeds
beneath my skin
knowing the light
needed for growth
comes from inside

perfect world

in a perfect world
we wouldn't
have to say goodbye
to our best memories
and the people
that made them special

fading good

the worst thing
about saying goodbye
is having to put aside
the best moments
and only focus
on the one at the end
that tore us apart

definition of happiness

your definition
of happiness
is different
than mine,
and that is okay.
we are not all
meant to live
the same life,
but we all deserve
to live happy.

built right

i'm walking away
from everything we built
because i am starting
to see the cracks
on the walls
that once stood so strong
i'm scared of waiting and hoping
that the roof won't crash down upon me
while letting my life go by
as i wait and wonder if i'll survive
for something that wasn't built
right to begin with

torn

so many sleepless nights
wasted away
for pondering the question
i am so scared to ask out loud.
"how can i walk away
and still keep myself whole
from something that built me
into what i stand today?"
i'm terrified of my life without you
just as much as i'm scared
knowing i'll continue
being unhappy if i stay.

the difference

you are perfect for me
but you are not my essence
of what i need
for there is a big difference in
love of my life
and a soulmate

process

as much as it hurts now
i know it needed to be done
as you know this
just as much as i
this pain will become growth
and wounds will turn into strength

dark spaces

you took my hand
and pulled me up
from the dark spaces
i called my home
for so many years
and while i enjoyed
your light
i felt suffocated
with this love
that turned poison
and i am desperate
to run away to my dark
where i can at least
be safe once again

funeral of hearts

what you call love
is more of a
funeral of hearts
than a
union of soul

ocean wave

just as the ocean
sends a wave
to crash on the shore
and then pulls it back
life is putting you down
till it feels like
you're coming undone.
it may seem bad now
but there is a plan for everything
and your deep fall
only means a higher rise.

blind

the worst thing
was not your
misinterpretation
of what love is
and the words and actions
you expressed by it
but me not knowing
my own self
being so blind
to think this is what
i deserve and need
and that it is okay
to be treated this way

<u>cost</u>

the cost of losing someone
is losing a part of yourself
how much your heart is open
determines how big of a piece
you are saying goodbye to

broken

darling,
show me your broken
and i'll kiss your scars
and prove to you
just how beautiful
they made you.

getting through this

i'm going to get through this.
no matter what happens
i will be okay
and i will rise above it all
because even if you
cut off my wings
and constrict me
to the ground
i will pick myself up
and walk until i find
a mountain high enough
to give me the sensation
of soaring among the clouds.
and when i scale that high peak
i will become free again
so my scars will born wings
and that person you cast aside
will become an angel.
and honey,
you have no idea
the love you created
just by refusing to give it
and the strength
that came from it.

wishing...

i wish upon a day
when you wake up
without dried up tears
from the night before
and your heart heavy
from words spoken
without a thought.
i wish upon
a beautiful morning for you
to wake up happy,
your heart stretched from love,
tears of laughter and joy
blessing your rosy cheeks.
to remember all the good
and forget all the bad,
to live life as free as a bird
without a care in the world.
i wish upon a day
when you refuse to go to sleep
fearing it may never be this good
ever again.

still rising

i wish for you to wake up one day
look at an old photo
and not recognize yourself
from all the
growth and strength
that fuels your
courage and determination.
to rise from all the shit
thrown your way.
you are way above the filth
of the past
and my dear,
you are still rising.

shining from within

let the light
shine from within
and you'll never
find yourself
walking in the dark.
focus on the positive
in your step
and good things
will greet you
on your journey.

cruel world

you were born
in a cruel world
so don't be fooled,
we are just as much
in the jungle
as the animals
fighting to survive
on a daily basis.
only difference,
one growls and hisses
when on defense
and ready to attack,
and the other
greets with a smile
while they stab you
in the back.

value

know your value
and the strength
residing within
and never let this
fucking world
or anyone in it
tear you apart

f*cked up place

this world
is a fucked up place
full of bullshiters
and deceivers,
but who am i to judge?
i call it a home
just as much
as everyone else
and yet,
i'm still waiting
for a brighter tomorrow
and hoping for someone
to prove me wrong.

saving myself

i know you're hurting
and i know you're tired
but i know the strength
you carry with you
deep down inside
and i hope
that one day
you'll wake up
and realize
that the only person
capable of saving you
is yourself

deep dug roots

that girl you mistreated

and cast aside

will pick herself up

and start to grow

roots dug so deep

of self-love and respect

that no one

can ever topple her down

life = videogame

if not anything,
life is like a videogame.
if you go through it
meeting some enemies
along the way
you are doing something right
and are on the right path.

<u>let go</u>

the only way to get rid of

the shit

from the past

is to focus

on the beauty

and opportunity

of the future

repressed love

how dare you
refuse to love
just because
you were
repressed by it

<u>losing myself</u>

don't spend your life
searching for love
only to realize
you lost yourself
along the way

write your chapters

life is too short
to listen to others
how to live happy
when the definition
of happiness
is subjected
to each individual,
so stop reading
the pages
of someone else's book.

wrong hands

find your balance
by staying in one piece.
the scale can only
be shifted by you
and no one else,
so stop handing
the power to people
that will abuse it.

haunted

i am still haunted
by a broken piece
from a once shattered heart,
and it hurts
living with this ghost
from the past
and as much
as it's easy
to move on
and accept it,
it's harder to forget
when it's something
that shaped you
and made you grow
from your past self.

out of luck

if you're looking
for an apology
for how i lived
you are out of luck
for all that i did
was merely survive you

self-investment

life will immediately
get better
when you stop
trying so hard
for people
who don't even
try for you
and put that energy
in yourself

<u>tonight</u>

tonight
we'll put more distance
between you and heartache
...
tonight
we'll put ourselves first
and practice self-love
...
tonight
we'll take the broken
and wear it like a crown
for the whole world to see
just how big of wings
our scars really have

reshaping

i'm not broken
i'm just reshaping
into something

better
bolder
brighter

half measures

don't expect to heal
in a place that loves you
only in half measures.
stray away from the toxic
and run to hands
that will nurture,
warmth that will heal,
soul that will ignite yours
and heart that will restart your
until they beat in unison.

hands of the moon

some nights i feel
that the only safe place
is in the hands of the moon
where i can pour my heart out
and let my thoughts roam free
scattered across the stars
wishing it could be so easy
to escape it all
and float among
my new infinite friends

<u>daydreamer</u>

she was a daydreamer
wishing for the clouds
to carry her heavy heart
and while she couldn't fly
she was brave enough
to reach deep down
and planted roots
withing herself
so she could grow abundantly
from the fire in her bones
and the love in her soul
to reach the heights
only experienced in her dreams

turn the page

i wish for you
to find the courage
and gather the strength
to rip the pages of your past
still remembering the torn remains
and write a new story
where your heart can create a home
and your soul finds peace

being me

i was withering away,
slowly fading into darkness
until i disappeared into my shadow
not knowing where it begins and i end.
and when the sun finally rose
after what felt like eternity
surrounded by nothing
but a crippling fear
that this can be my forever,
the light washed away my sorrows
and carved the black from my heart
like a wave crashing on the beach.
i was pulled back into safe hands
so i could start again,
given another opportunity
to be let back in
and learn from my mistakes,
to let go, to move on,
to grow, to accept,
to empty and to fill
the right places of me
so my soul can be free
and i can start being me.

<u>new me</u>

let go of the broken
but remember the scars
that the pain caused
and know
that hearts break down
not open
and what is left inside
rebuilds the walls around
stronger and better
so the next pain that comes
can knock or hit
but cannot pierce through
the strong structure
you have built
that we now call
a new you

wrong places

don't go looking
for a rose in me
and be disappointed
when you find a wildflower
...
i grow in unsteady places
bloom in heavy situations
survived uneasy combinations
finding me takes patience
as i'm planted under constellations
i may not meet your expectation
but deep down i know
i am a beautiful creation

dark places

i was looking for myself
in other people
and still question
why i felt lost
until the day came
when i looked at myself
and reached deep down inside
and found what i was looking for
among all the mess
in those dark places
it may not be pretty
but at least you know
it is true

lessons

autumn has taught me
the importance
of letting go
if we want to grow
the moon has shown me
that even in darkness
we can shine bright
and even when half full
we can look beautiful
the sea has taught me
that you can fight
as much as you can
but sometimes
it's better to let go
and let the current carry you

piece of you/part of them

it is hard letting go
especially when knowing
you are not only
letting go of them
but a piece of you
that you gave away
for it to become
part of them as well

left behind

it is hard walking away from you
but it's even harder walking away
from myself
when all i see in you
are the endless possibilities
of us together
while knowing
those are alternative universes
that do not apply to our reality
so i stand here
broken and alone
not knowing how to move on
when fearing that the part of me
that goes with you
can never be replaced
and i'll forever remain empty
endlessly searching for something
to fill the dark space you left behind
and crying when knowing
i already had it
but had to leave it behind

fight for a voice

i'm so tired
going through every day
exactly the same
fighting for a voice
to make a stand for myself
that my life is mine to live
and fight those who dictate
how i am in the wrong
and how it should be lived
when they don't even know me
yet want to make me
a part of the crowd
that is rather a copy than an original
just because it's easy and safe

<u>it's okay</u>

it's okay to be single if you choose
it's okay to have a partner if you wish
it's okay to start a family
and it's okay to be left alone
as long as you are the one
making that decision
and do not enforce it
onto others
but let them live
their lives the way
it makes them happy
and leave them the hell alone
so they can pursue that
without any judgment or pressure
let life be lived
because there are many ways
to reach happiness
you just have to find your own
and do not feel bad
if you find only yourself
walking on it
it won't matter when you reach the end

locking you out

you're not going to hear me apologize
for building my walls
just to get away from your shit
and lock you outside
where your poison
can't reach me
anymore

<u>brave</u>

be brave my dear
and take the first step
but don't you worry
if you don't have
anyone to follow.
be like the first
flower of spring,
worth of admiration
that paves a way
for others to follow
in her step
to grow bigger
and brighter
behind her
until we transform the world
and find magic
in our colorful petals.

arms of fate

just because you can't see
where you're going
does not mean
you are lost.
close your eyes
and put yourself
in the arms of fate.
let the current of life
carry you on your way
and soon you'll find yourself
standing right where you need to be.

thank you

i want to thank you
for breaking me
as you gave the opportunity
for the toxic to be released
and the light
to find her way
through the cracks
into my shattered heart
once again

one day

one day you'll find
your PATIENCE
your PEACE
your SANITY
your HAPPINESS
your STRENGTH
your VOICE
and i feel sorry for every
poor fool that will try to
CONTROL you
MISTREAT you
MANIPULATE you
USE you
and HURT you...

.

.

.

... but not really

home

there will come a day
when you'll find a home
the moment you stop
looking for it
and it won't be a place
but rather a person
that will always find room
for all your carried baggage
as they will grow with you
until you fill in
the empty spaces
of each other
finally becoming whole
and finally being
home...

strength within

in those times
when it's hard to breathe
and your walls are crumbling down
when the pain becomes too real
and you feel yourself fading away
just sit softly
and think deeply
fill that mind
with words you would want to hear
from the one your heart
beats the hardest for
and watch those hard moments
retract into those dark spaces
where they can't hurt you anymore

weight of the heart

i know it is hard
this weight you carry in your heart
like an anchor holding you down
sinking your soul
until it gets harder to breathe
when you feel like drowning
and i wish i could take
away this burden from you
but it's not mine to carry
and the only hands that can lift it
are the same ones wrapped
around your heart
keeping it from completely
coming apart
so find the strength
and fight the current
until you bring your
sinking ship back to the shore

focus on yourself

stop compromising
your happiness
just to ignite his

mask

i hate for you
to wear that heavy mask
for so long
that an extra layer
starts to grow
and you end up believing
the very same lie
that kept you
from falling apart
and begins to root deep
and becomes a part
of your identity

her hero

she was standing here broken
and yet
she didn't let anyone
heal her wounds
kiss her scars
and mend her heart
as she knew
this sadness was hers to carry
and the only hero she needed
was living inside her all along

<u>hardest thing</u>

it is not about
your heart being broken
that is the hardest thing
but the uncertainty
that follows soon after
when you feel lost in the world
doubting yourself
as much as everything
around you
when you're unsure of yourself
and the future ahead
but that is the time
when you pick yourself up
and grow stronger
...thicker
...harder
when you find yourself again
in all the million little broken pieces
where everyone saw damage
you saw an opportunity to build
and with every laid brick
you created something in yourself
that can never be torn down again

sick & tired

i am so sick and tired
listening to others
saying what i need
to be happy
while they are still
figuring out
what the hell
do they want
from their own damn life

false expectations

the worst thing
about having
a good heart
is that you assume
everyone else's is the same
so when you give yours
foolish and unknowing
in cold hand
thinking they will
nurture with warmth
and love with care
you find yourself
in realization
of the best lesson
that a lie
is often disguised
as something beautiful
and speaks words
sweet like honey
yet poisons you
with the venomous tongue
that bring you down
and actions
that tears you apart
one small piece at a time
until the day comes
when you are completely broken
and too late to stop the damage

sinking ship

you are broken,
a sinking ship
lost in the ocean,
and it's okay
to feel that way
as long as you know
it is only temporary
because sometimes
staying and fighting
does more damage
than letting go.
so choose your battles wisely
and remember
to breathe today
so you can live tomorrow
and don't worry
for things out of your control.

lying to myself

stop pretending
that those past heartaches
are anything but normal.
stop lying
in your pictures and captions
posted on social media
hiding behind a smile
you and i both know is fake.
so stop telling yourself
it is what it is
just to get yourself to sleep
and start admitting to yourself
that something is wrong
and finally doing something about it.
pretending the problem
doesn't exist
only hides it
but to erase it from existence
you have to fight those demons
and deal with them
until they vanish.
you can bullshit to the world
but don't lie to yourself.

healing

healing begins
the moment
we accept
what happened
and forgive
ourselves

better days

stay strong, beautiful creature
better days are on the horizon
and with it
a reason to bless us
with your smile once again

clawing for survival

her mind destroyed,
heart shattered,
soul torn,
spirit broken,
and yet she still fights
with the same ferocity
she did at the start
cause she may be tired
but she is strong.
keeping a lioness
inside her chest
kept her alive,
clawing for survival
in a world
that doesn't believe in her
and only beats her down,
but she still takes
all that pain
and casts out the dark
transforming it into triumph.

self-love

be kind to yourself,
your love
is the only constant
you will get
in this life.

not deserving of your story

how many sleepless nights,
how many heartaches,
how many tears shed
will it take
to finally realize
the fault in your step?
the error in your way.
to stop giving your heart
to hands which are blind
to the value they hold.
the ones that don't deserve
to be a part
of your story.

<u>ends here</u>

my only regret
was wasting years
warming souls
with my heart
while i
was freezing
from the hailstorm
they called love
...
but this ends here...

making room

when i talk
about my past
i am making room
for you
in my future

deprivation

how dare you
refuse to give love
just because you were
deprived of it

necessity

no matter what
always put yourself first.
it's not selfish
it's necessary.

The End

a letter:

No matter how much life brings you down, wraps its claws around your neck and throws you into darkness; you will gather your strength, pick yourself up and move on. Admitting defeat is not an option. Never. Not for you.

When the world goes dark again, you must be the light that overcomes that darkness. You must smile despite everything what is happening around you. The world is in dire need of soft hands and kind souls.

So be those hands. Be that softness. Be kind. Be gentle. Be everything that the world is telling you not to be and walk in the opposite direction of everything that it's trying to turn you into.

You are strong. You are able. I know you're tired, but you're a survivor.

Sing now, my dear. Sing from the heart and let everyone know that even the saddest songs can be beautiful and worth listening to. Make your voice heard. They can't ignore you forever.

As you sing, you are changing the world, one exhale at a time.

Love yourself and be kind to one another.

With love,
  c.r. Elliott

Printed in Great Britain
by Amazon